VISUAL AID

VISUAL AID

ANNIE LEIBOVITZ

ROBERT MAPPLETHORPE

DAVID BAILEY

MATTHEW ROLSTON

SHEILA METZNER

HERB RITTS

SNOWDON

GREG GORMAN

ANDY WARHOL

PANTHEON BOOKS

New York

Edited by

JAMES DANZIGER

Foreword by

CORNELL CAPA

Designed by

LLOYD ZIFF

Library of Congress Cataloging-in-Publication Data
Visual aid.
1. Photography—Portraits.   2. Celebrities—
Portraits.   I. Leibovitz, Annie, 1949–   .
II. Danziger, James, 1953—   .   III. Capa, Cornell.
TR681.F3V57   1986   779'.2'0922   86-42622
ISBN 0-394-55664-X

The year is 1986, and here is a new book of photographs with nine portfolios by famed contemporary photographers.

Twenty years ago, occasioned by the moral fervor against the Vietnam War and the violence and killings in the Civil Rights struggle in the United States, I was moved to put together *The Concerned Photographer* book and exhibit. It showed the work of six photographers, four of them dead, whose subjects and images reflected their concern for humankind—among them images of famine in India, the ravages of war and its effects on the survivors, and the Civil Rights movement.

Now, I am asked to write an introduction for a book of photographs with another cause in mind: hunger and homelessness in Africa and America. The fine photographs in this book do not depict these themes, they are instead memorable portraits of the contemporary stars of popular culture by highly respected photographers in their fields. With the publication of this book these photographers are contributing their best to alleviate the problems that now confront us all.

The causes of the decades, the sensibilities of the participants are different. Three things remain constant: the desperate need of humankind, the capacity of photographs to move souls to act, and photographers to help.

Perhaps we have learned that it is the constancy of the heart that is our best hope for survival.

CORNELL CAPA
MAY 1986, NEW YORK

I f 1985 was the year when charity became an event, then with a bit of luck 1986 will be remembered as the year it became a process. *Visual Aid,* whose proceeds will be used to fight hunger and homelessness, was inspired by the concerned musicians who came together in Band Aid and U.S.A. for Africa. This time, however, the contributors are photographers who could best be described as the most exciting names in editorial photography covering the worlds of entertainment, fashion, and style. The images in *Visual Aid* are the best of these photographers' recent work, all previously unpublished in book form. The proceeds are being administered by U.S.A. for Africa and divided between lifesaving programs in Africa and America. Whatever the ironies of the contemporary trend of celebrities as galvanizers of public awareness on social issues, the results speak for themselves. A recent *New York Times* article stated that seven million lives have been saved as a result of the efforts of Live Aid and U.S.A. for Africa, but the need is constant. Thus *Visual Aid.*

It was our hope to assemble a volume that lovers of photography would be eager to have while at the same time knowing that they were contributing to a good cause. With the ninety photographs selected for this book, I think we have a pretty impressive representation of the state of the art.

Annie Leibovitz, whose photographs over the last decade have redefined the way we look at color portraiture, has put together a portfolio of her most striking images. In Robert Mapplethorpe's pictures we see the life within the formality of his fine-art approach to photography. David Bailey's photographs represent a stunning example of grace under pressure, having been taken in a makeshift studio erected behind the stage at the London Live Aid concert; while Matthew Rolston's work combines the classicism of the glamour photography of the thirties with the coolness of the eighties. In Sheila Metzner's pictures we see how one of today's top fashion photographers brings her sensual eye to all her subjects from portraits to still lifes. Herb Ritts's pictures combine the elegance of fashion photography with the immediacy of reportage. Snowdon's portfolio shows his famous range and versatility, while Greg Gorman captures the spirit of today's most popular stars with his bold and graphic eye. We end with a rarely seen selection of the Polaroid pictures Andy Warhol takes on his drugstore "Sure Shot" camera, which form the basis of his larger painted portraits. They confirm—as do all the pictures in this book—that in photography it is the artist who counts, and that the process of photography can preserve life in many ways.

A book like this could not be put together without the help of many people, but I would like to thank above all the book's photographers, designer, and their assistants for their generosity and time: Annie Leibovitz and Carol Le Flufy, Robert Mapplethorpe and Tina Summerlin, Sheila Metzner and Nell Gutman, David Bailey and Sarah Lane, Lord Snowdon and Evelyn Humphries, Greg Gorman and Rob Platz, Matthew Rolston and Bill Swan, Herb Ritts, Andy Warhol, Lloyd Ziff, Greg Wakabayashi, and Richard Pandiscio.

My thanks to the many celebrities who are featured in this book; to Wendy Goldwyn of Pantheon for her friendship and tireless support of the project from inception to completion; and to Diana Edkins of Condé Nast, David Fahey of Los Angeles's G. Ray Hawkins Gallery, and Philippe Garner of Sotheby's—a priceless brain trust who became, in effect, the book's editorial advisers.

I would also like to thank Gael Love for her help when the going got tough, together with Marc Balet of *Interview,* and Tina Brown and Ruth Ansel of *Vanity Fair*—they were the editors and art directors who originally commissioned many of the photographs in this book. Thanks as well to Anna Winand, Richard Stolley, Doris O'Neil, Marie Schumann, Leslie Nolen, Mary Ann Morris, Cynthia Cathcart, Diane Spoto, William Rayner, Beatrix Miller, Lillie Davies, Mark Boxer, Michael Roberts, Lucinda Chambers, Michael Rand, Stephen Wood, Jane Sarkin, Vincent Fremont, Jimmy Moffat, Mary Ellen Mark, Horst, Kendall Conrad, and last but not least Robert Pledge.

It should also be mentioned that everyone involved with this book contributed their own expenses, time, and work, without reimbursement. In this way we were assured that every penny raised would go directly to charity.

JAMES DANZIGER
SEPTEMBER 1986, NEW YORK

VISUAL AID

ANNIE LEIBOVITZ

DARYL HANNAH   GREG LOUGANIS

DIANE KEATON

WHOOPI GOLDBERG

ANJELICA HUSTON

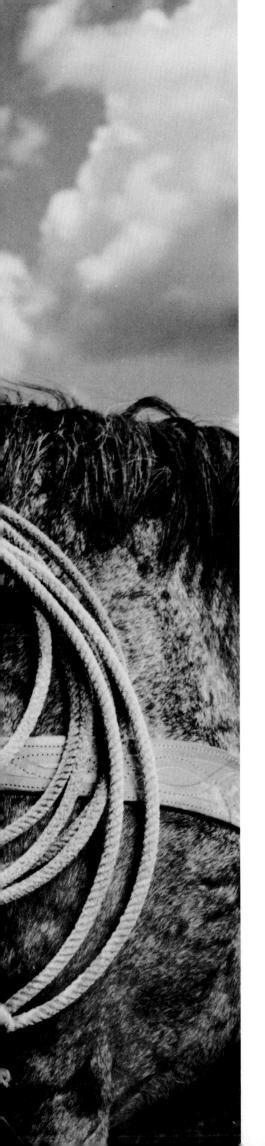

SAM SHEPARD

MALCOLM McLAREN   JERRY HALL

MICK JAGGER

ROBERT MAPPLETHORPE

RAE DAWN CHONG

PHILIP GLASS

NORMAN MAILER

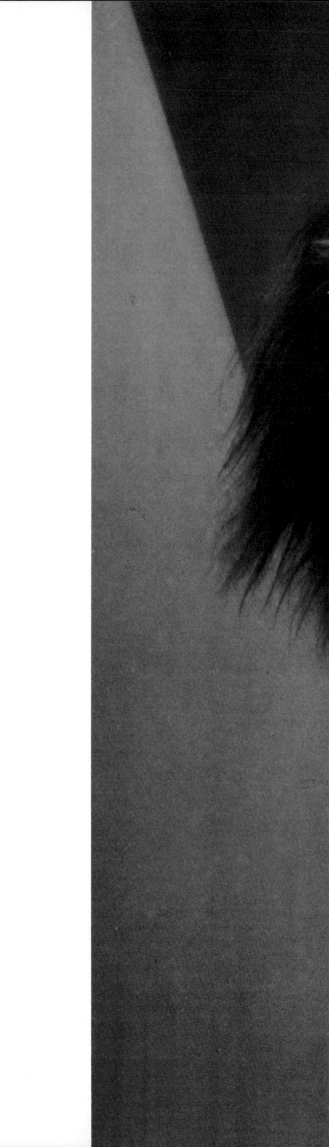

RICHARD GERE and VALERIE KAPRISKY

PATTI HANSEN and THEODORA DUPREE RICHARDS   AMY IRVING and MAX SPIELBERG

KATHLEEN TURNER

LISA LYON   GREGORY HINES

SONIA BRAGA

DAVID BAILEY

BOB GELDOF

ELVIS COSTELLO

PHIL COLLINS

MIDGE URE

BRYAN FERRY

STING

DAVID BOWIE

PAUL and LINDA McCARTNEY

ELTON JOHN and GEORGE MICHAEL

PETE TOWNSHEND

MATTHEW ROLSTON

JANE FONDA

TIMOTHY HUTTON

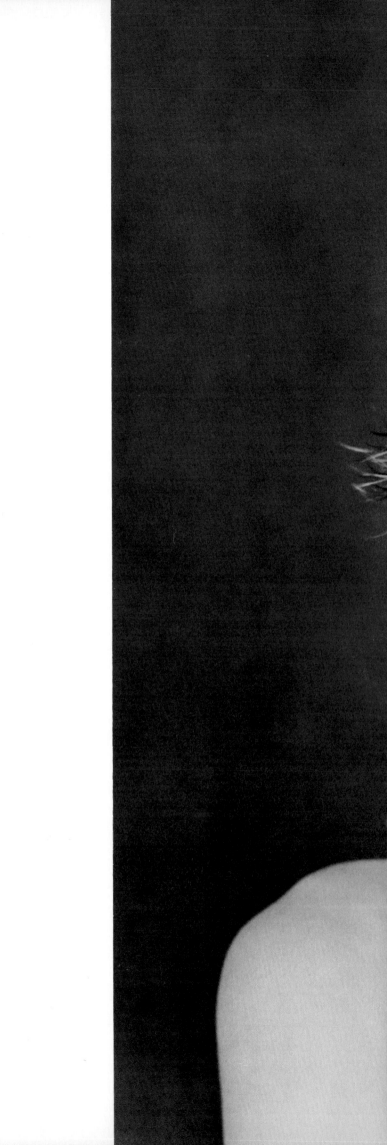

MOLLY RINGWALD

"Sloth" and "Envy," from the series KELLY LeBROCK *and the Seven Deadly Sins*

STEVEN SPIELBERG

JOAN JETT

CYNDI LAUPER   MICHAEL JACKSON

SHIRLEY MACLAINE

SHEILA METZNER

MIA SARA

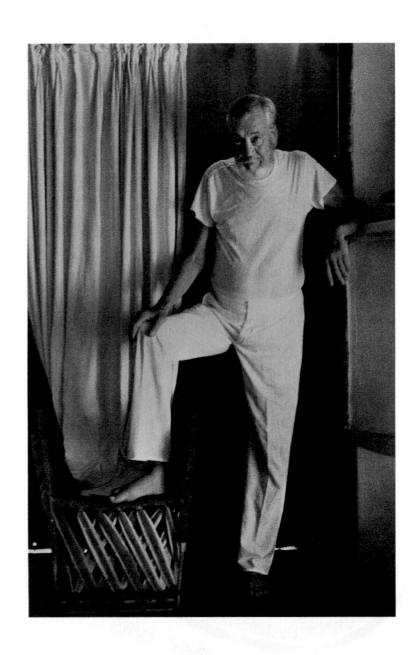

JOHN HUSTON

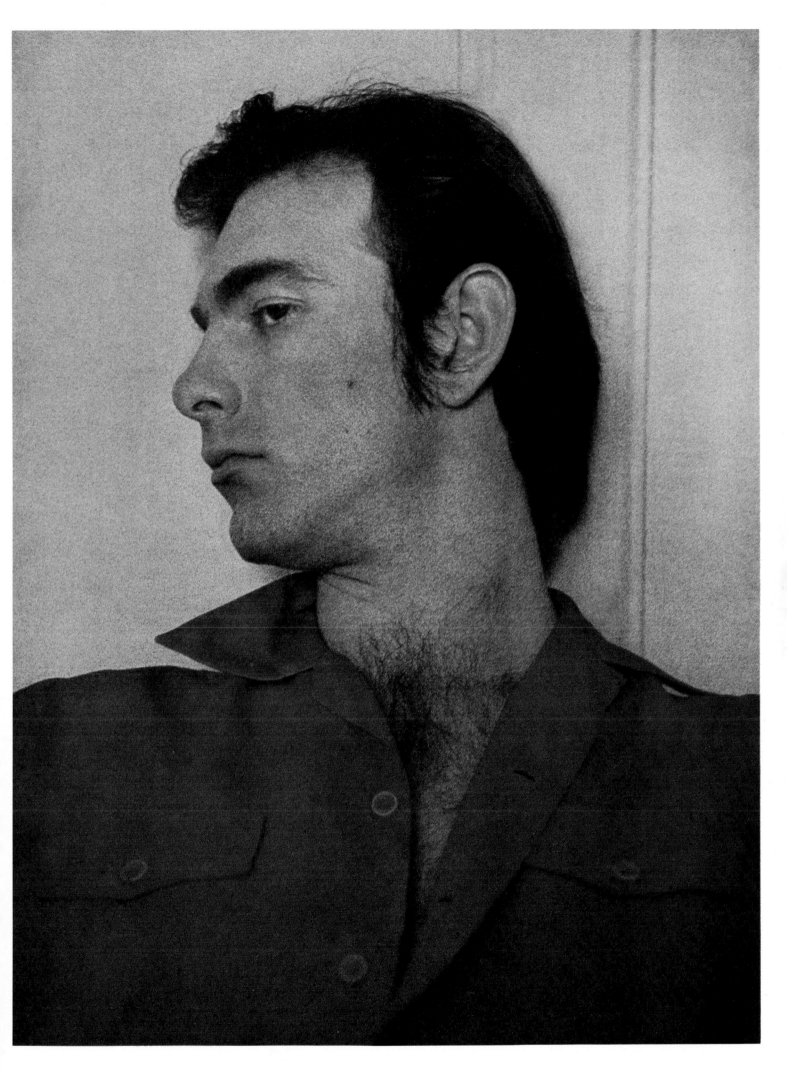

JOHN SAYLES

ROSEMARY McGROTHA

Fashion *(BRITISH VOGUE)*

BROOKE SHIELDS

THE METROPOLITAN INSURANCE BUILDING, NEW YORK CITY

Shoe *(VOGUE)*

MOLLY RINGWALD

JEANNE MOREAU

HERB RITTS

MEL GIBSON

SEAN PENN and MADONNA

MADONNA

TOM CRUISE

MICHELLE PFEIFFER

ANDIE MacDOWELL

KARINA

BOB PARIS "Mr. Olympia"

RICHARD GERE in *The Cotton Club*

SNOWDON

NANCY REAGAN

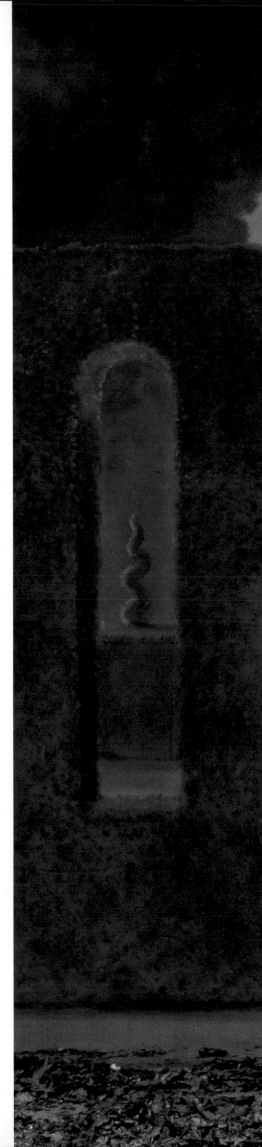

ISABELLE PASCO *(BRITISH VOGUE)*

MIKHAIL BARYSHNIKOV AND ISABELLA ROSSELLINI

POPOV

ALLIUM SICCULUM *(BRITISH VOGUE)*   THE NATTERJACK TOAD *(BRITISH VOGUE)*

PAUL McCARTNEY

TINA TURNER

GREG GORMAN

ARNOLD SCHWARZENEGGER

MATT DILLON

KIM BASINGER

TOM WAITS

GRACE JONES

DAVID BOWIE

MICKEY ROURKE

ALEXANDER GODUNOV

DOLPH LUNDGREN

JESSICA LANGE, GOLDIE HAWN, JANE FONDA,
SALLY FIELD, and BARBRA STREISAND

TINA CHOW

JOAN COLLINS

JEAN-MICHEL BASQUIAT

TOM SEAVER

GEORGIA O'KEEFFE

DENNIS HOPPER

LIZA MINNELLI

ARNOLD SCHWARZENEGGER

CARLY SIMON

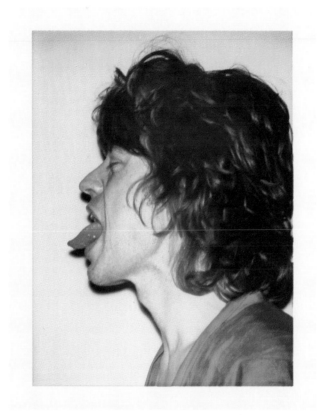

MICK JAGGER

ANNIE LEIBOVITZ

"A thing that you see in my pictures," Annie Leibovitz said in an interview several years ago, "is that I was not afraid to fall in love with these people." As chief photographer for *Rolling Stone* and then as *Vanity Fair*'s photographer-at-large she has combined the commitment of emotion with state-of-the-art technique to produce a remarkably consistent and original body of work. Leibovitz began photographing while at college and at the age of twenty took her portfolio to Jann Wenner at *Rolling Stone.* Her first assignment was to photograph John Lennon, and within a month her work was on the cover of the magazine. The long and fruitful relationship lasted for thirteen years, until Leibovitz left to help start up the new *Vanity Fair.* From her new base she is dispatched around the world.

ROBERT MAPPLETHORPE

Robert Mapplethorpe is the fine-art photographer who brought the mainstream over to him rather than cross the road. Soft-spoken, always a little wary, he records subjects famous, floral, geometric, and sexual, with equal intensity. He is also a sculptor, set designer, and collector of objects ranging from statues of Lucifer to 1960s Swedish glassware. He took up photography in 1975 and shocked the art world with his starkly unambiguous photographs of homosexual and sado-masochistic ritual. Soon magazines from *Vogue* to the *London Sunday Times* were assigning him to photograph the famous. Yet nothing seems to turn his head. When you visit his studio he is more likely to be excited by a grimacing portrait he has just taken of an unknown weightlifter or a photograph of a flower than a call from Hollywood asking him to photograph the latest superstar.

DAVID BAILEY

The original mod photographer of the 1960s, David Bailey first brought fashion and portrait photography in touch with pop sensibility. In 1975 when Bailey was branching out into film and television, Cecil Beaton described him as "a dark Raeburnesque boy, with lots of picturesque gear and an eye for beautiful girls" and expressed the hope that he "would not branch out into too many distracting diversions." He did not. Deeply dedicated to the medium of photography,

Bailey has curated shows, collected photographs, published books, and led the way for photographers other than photojournalists to get involved in political and humanitarian causes. He was one of the very first photographers to become aware of the famine in Africa and has remained committed to the cause, exhibiting his pictures of Ethiopia and donating his photographs of the Live Aid musicians to raise funds around the world.

MATTHEW ROLSTON

Thirty years old, Matthew Rolston began to see his work published while still in art school and quickly made a name for himself when his luxurious portraits of movie stars were first published in *Interview* magazine. Dubbed one of ''the new glamorists'' (along with Herb Ritts and Greg Gorman) because of his allegiance to the tradition of the Hollywood studio photographers of the thirties, Matthew Rolston is the only one of the three not to be put off by the name. His influences are George Hurrel and Josef von Sternberg. His shoots are miniature productions in themselves, often employing a team of half a dozen hairdressers, makeup artists, and assistants. His concern is not so much to bring out the central truth of his sitters but to bring out the best in them—which is not to say this approach cannot be just as revealing.

SHEILA METZNER

Sheila Metzner, a successful art director at the advertising agency Doyle Dane Bernbach in the late sixties, decided after the birth of her first child to become a photographer. She knew what sort of pictures she wanted to take but first had to find out how to take them. Her concerns were not particularly fashionable at the time—quietness, order, beauty—but she was confident in her vision, and after three years of quietly taking pictures of her family and friends, learning and refining her technique, she took her portfolio to John Szarkowski, director of photography at the Museum of Modern Art. Szarkowski immediately acquired a print and put it into his seminal ''Mirrors and Windows'' show, thus launching a career that has taken Metzner from photographing fashion for *Vogue* to shooting the space shuttle for *Rolling Stone.* Today Metzner shows at the G. Ray Hawkins Gallery in Los Angeles and at Daniel Wolf in New York and is one of the best-selling contemporary photographers in the world.

HERB RITTS

Herb Ritts is a young photographer who has recently found his form. A latecomer to the profession, at the age of twenty-eight Ritts left the family business (manufacturing acrylic furniture) to take up photography. Within three years his pictures were being published in *Interview, Rolling Stone, Vanity Fair,* and *British Vogue.* His initial interest was in portraiture, but after a year in Italy Ritts had become an accomplished fashion photographer; his current work often shows the influence of both disciplines. Although based in Los Angeles, Ritts's modern and almost antiglamour style is much in demand on the East Coast and in Europe, and he is one of a select group of photographers whose distinctive look has allowed their personal and commercial work to be virtually indistinguishable.

SNOWDON

Photojournalist, portraitist, inventor, architect, film-maker, conservationist, lobbyist on behalf of the rights of the disabled, Snowdon wears many hats. His interest in photography began when he was a schoolboy, however, and it has remained his one consuming passion. His boundless curiosity and willingness to experiment mark his style. He loves simplicity yet revels in certain trick effects. He can happily use the same background cloth in his studio for years, and yet use it to produce totally different but appropriate portraits of the royal family and up-and-coming film stars. He claims not to take photography seriously. "It is not one of the fine arts," he has said. "The good thing about photography is that it can be easily enjoyed." But he has published eight photography books, exhibited his pictures around the world, and directed a widely acclaimed series on photography for BBC.

GREG GORMAN

Greg Gorman grew up in the midwest and studied cinematography at the University of Southern California before starting work as a photojournalist. Moving quickly into the film world, he went from being a location photographer to shooting studio portraits and posters for all the major studios. (*Tootsie, The Big Chill,* and *Down and Out in Beverly Hills* are among his most famous commissions.) As testament to what must also be a remarkably diplomatic disposition, Gorman has become the de facto personal photographer of stars ranging from Barbra Streisand to Dustin Hoffman, Bette Midler, and David Bowie. His most personal work, however, is done for *Interview* magazine, where what he terms his black-and-white "environmental portraits" have been appearing for the last five years.

ANDY WARHOL

"My idea of a good picture is one that's in focus and of a famous person," says Andy Warhol. This notwithstanding, Warhol was one of the first modern artists to fully absorb the language of photography. From his early Marilyn Monroe paintings to his disaster series to his current portraits, photographs form the basis of his work. As a photographer Warhol is deceptively brilliant. His *paparazzi*-style snapshots have been collected in two books, *Exposures* and *America*. They show his eye for the decisive moment to be spontaneous, socially and politically perceptive, and a little wicked. His Polaroid portraits would seem simple were they not in most cases definitive portraits of the sitters. Andy Warhol favors small autofocus and cheap instant cameras.

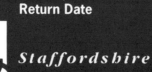